CHRIS PACKHAM

AMAZING ANIMAL
JOURNEYS

ILLUSTRATED BY JASON COCKCROFT

RED
SHED

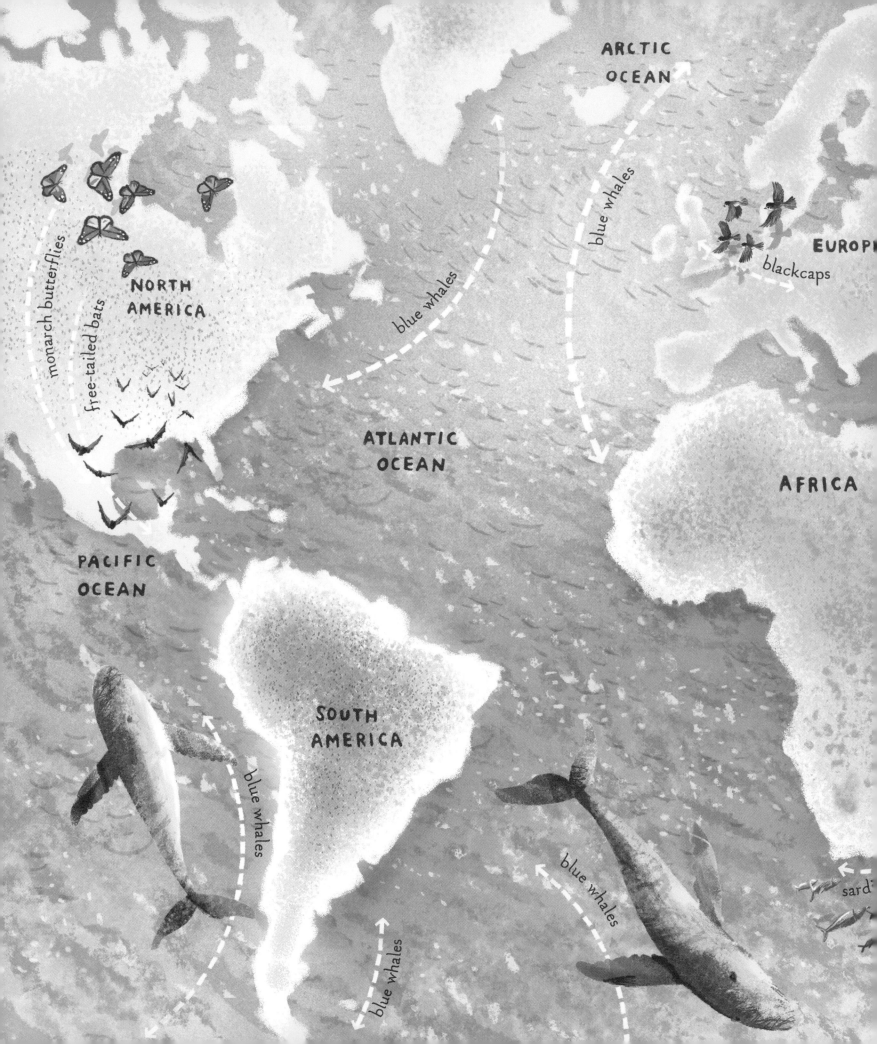

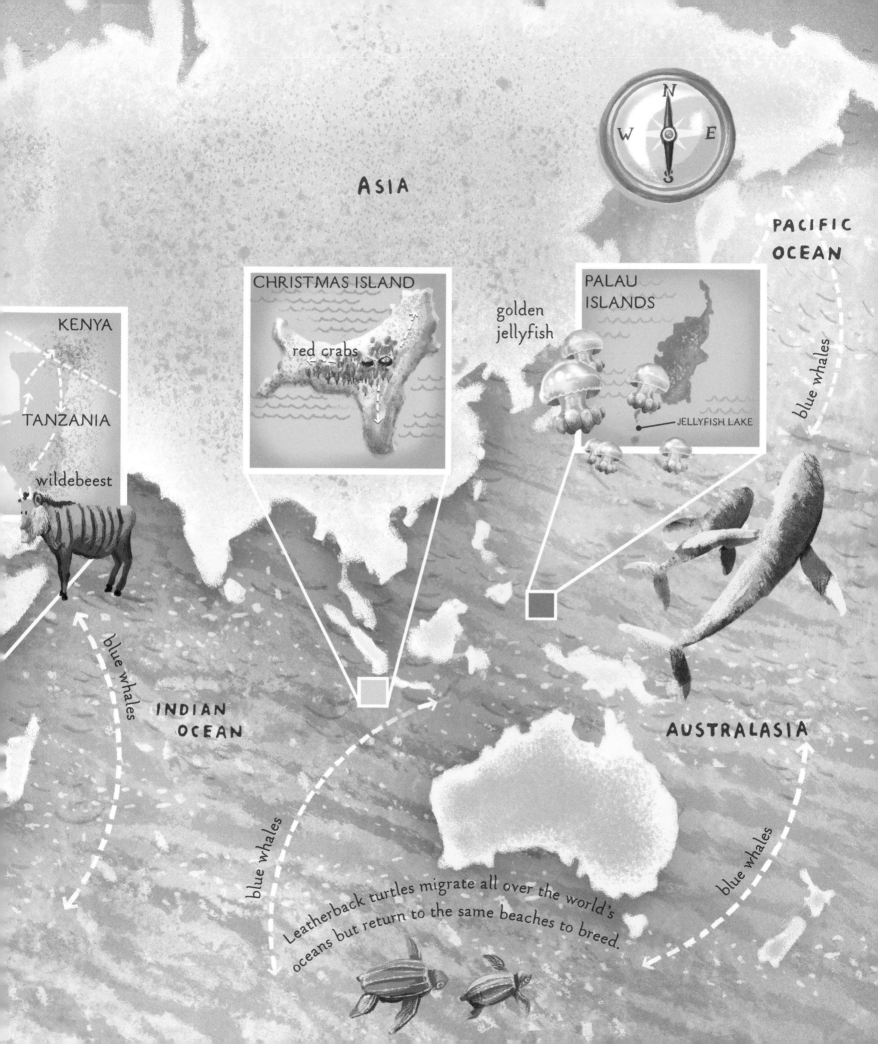

ASIA

N
W · E
S

PACIFIC OCEAN

KENYA

TANZANIA

wildebeest

CHRISTMAS ISLAND

red crabs

golden jellyfish

PALAU ISLANDS

JELLYFISH LAKE

blue whales

blue whales

INDIAN OCEAN

AUSTRALASIA

blue whales

blue whales

blue whales

Leatherback turtles migrate all over the world's oceans but return to the same beaches to breed.

Every year, billions of animals move from
one part of our planet to another.

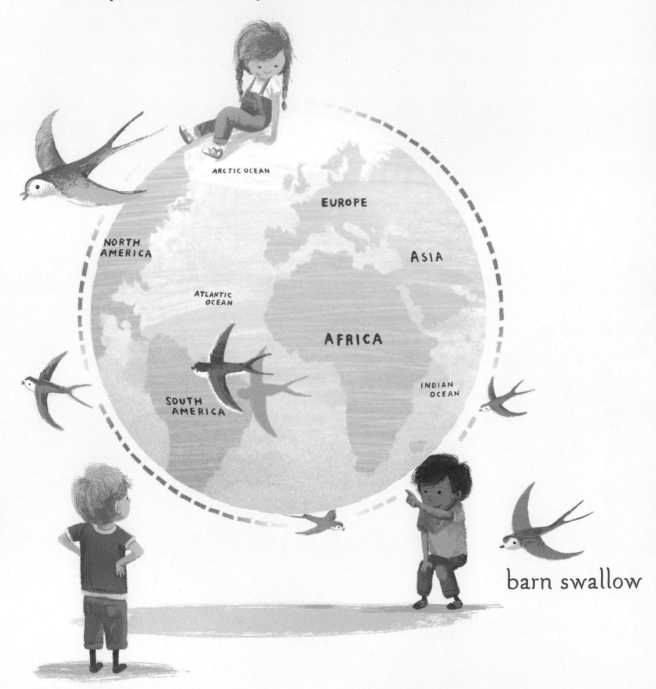

barn swallow

Birds, mammals, reptiles, amphibians,
fish and insects fly, run or swim around
Earth and this is known as **MIGRATION**.

Some migrate south in the winter
to avoid the cold and to be
sure of finding enough
food to survive
until the
spring.

Bewick's swan

Other animals travel to find mates or the
best places to breed and have their young.

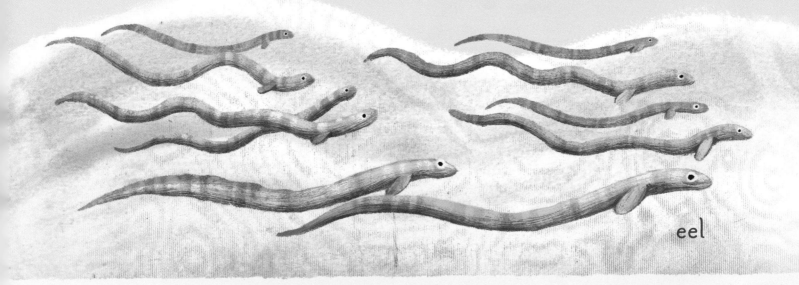

eel

red deer

Not all animals migrate massive distances or in huge numbers, some only come down from the mountains to the seaside . . .

. . . or move from the countryside into towns.

pied wagtail

But wherever you live you will
be able to see migrating animals.

barn swallow

Would you like to meet some
of the masters of migration?

harbour seal

Everything about the **BLUE WHALE** is big!
It's the largest creature to have ever lived
on Earth and it has a big appetite too!

Cold polar seas swarm with
animal life, and every day
the adults can each eat more
than three tonnes of food.

They have to migrate to warmer
tropical waters to give birth,
so the young whales don't get too
cold. But don't worry, the little ones
grow quickly and in spring the whole
family heads back for a massive meal!

SARDINES are small fish that travel in big numbers! Shoals of billions swim up the coast of Africa, but an awful lot end up in the stomachs of hungry whales.

Fishermen catch sardines too,
and because so many get caught in their
nets, these fish have begun to disappear.

This is bad news for the animals that
eat them, especially the poor whales!

A seawater lake on an island in the Pacific Ocean is home to **GOLDEN JELLYFISH**. Every day, millions of these animals swim from one end of the lake to the other and back again. So it's a very short migration . . . but without it they would all die.

The jellyfish follow the Sun because they have tiny plant-like algae living inside them that get energy from sunshine. It's this energy that keeps the jellyfish alive.

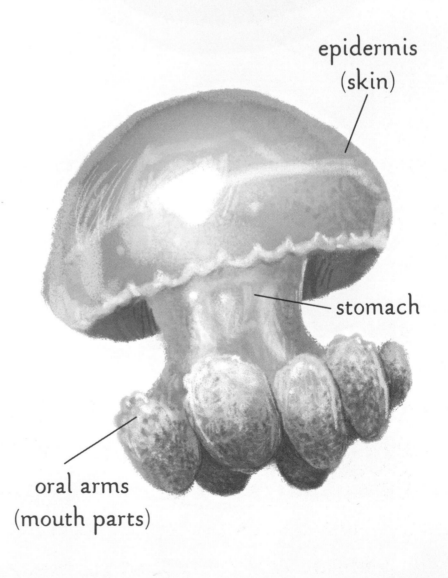

epidermis (skin)

stomach

oral arms (mouth parts)

Jellyfish are also the favourite food of some extraordinary reptiles – the **LEATHERBACK TURTLES!**

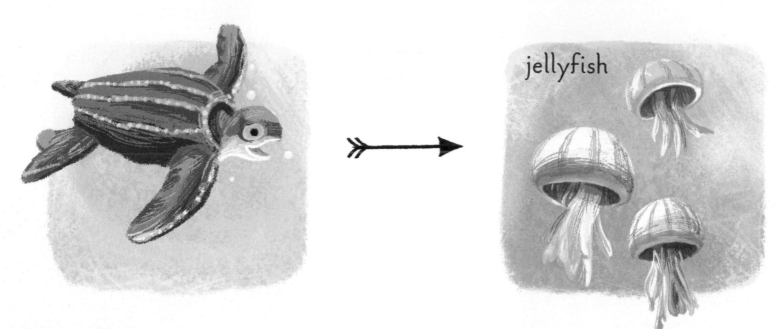

jellyfish

Every few years they paddle back to a special beach to breed, using a strange third 'eye' on the top of their head as a compass to help them find their way.

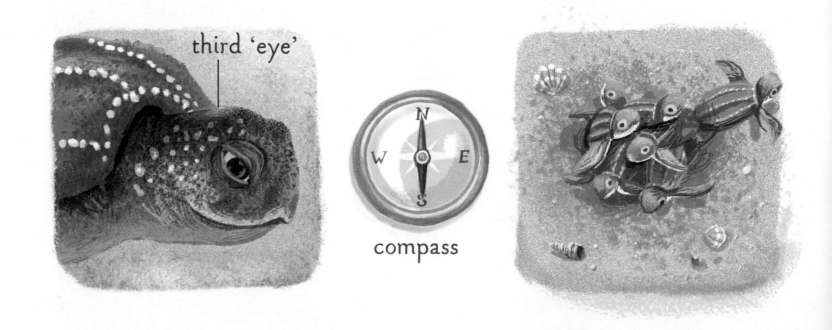

third 'eye'

compass

They choose beaches that are safe and have shallow, sandy shores that the turtles can climb and dig their nests into.

There is never snow on Christmas Island as it's in the warm Indian Ocean, but once a year when heavy rain falls, millions of **RED CRABS** scuttle out of the forest and down to the sea to breed.

The crabs cover the roads and can puncture car tyres with their tough shells if people drive over them.

Special 'crab wardens' help the crabs cross and get safely to the sea.

Migrating animals face other dangers too – they
need to watch out for other creatures that eat them!
WILDEBEEST roam in huge herds on the flat,
grassy savannas of Africa.

Because wildebeest soon eat all the grass, they must migrate to new spots so their young ones can find plenty of food.

lion

This is a very perilous journey as there are many animals waiting for them.

hyena

cheetah

crocodile

Some, such as crocodiles, have been waiting a year for this chance of a meal.

Where there's plenty of food, some animals will gather in mega-massive numbers. In a cave in Texas, USA, there are 20 million **FREE-TAILED BATS!**

Each night they all fly out to eat tonnes
of moths, beetles and other insects,
and in winter they all migrate
south from the USA to find
the warmer weather that
these insects like too.

Staying warm is very important to many animals, but how can something as tiny and fragile as a **MONARCH BUTTERFLY** flutter all the way from the cold of Canada to the heat of Mexico?

It's because they have powerful wings to fly high in the sky and faster than you can run.

The butterflies go all the way to the mountains of Mexico for the winter.

antennae

We think their antennae tell them which way to go. They are like a built-in compass.

Until recently many birds would fly to Africa for the winter. However due to climate change, some birds such as **BLACKCAPS** from central Europe now visit Britain.

The changing climate looks like it will be having a big effect on migration all over the world . . . maybe in your lifetime some animals will stop travelling altogether and others will start their own remarkable journeys!

In spring blackcaps that spend the winter in Britain return home first, get the best spots and survive better than other birds that fly south.

DISCOVER MORE

BARN SWALLOWS

Before people understood migration they thought that swallows spent the winter resting in mud at the bottom of ponds! The truth was revealed in 1912, when a bird that was tagged in the UK with a numbered ring around its leg was caught in South Africa.

BEWICK'S SWANS

These birds migrate in family groups and when they arrive in Russia to spend the winter there, they still stick together. Sometimes they even meet up with their offspring from previous years.

BLACKCAPS

Blackcaps feed on insects in the summer but switch to feeding on berries in the winter. This is why they can stay in cooler places instead of migrating to warmer places.

BLUE WHALES

Blue whales grow up to 30 metres long and can weigh 170 tonnes (about the weight of 170 large family cars). They give birth to young the same size as a hippopotamus! When the blue whales migrate to warmer waters where they breed, there isn't a lot of food there so the adults don't eat much for several months.

CHRISTMAS ISLAND RED CRABS

Christmas Island young crabs hide in burrows in the forests for about five years until it's time for them to breed. Once a year when heavy rain falls, the crabs all come out at the same time.

EELS

For thousands of years, no one knew where eels went to breed. It wasn't until 1922, when a Danish professor found baby eels in the Sargasso Sea in the Atlantic Ocean, that the mystery was solved.

FREE-TAILED BATS

Most free-tailed bats migrate about 1,500 kilometres from the USA to Mexico in the winter. This isn't the longest animal migration, but they can fly very high – about 3 kilometres up in the air.

GOLDEN JELLYFISH

Jellyfish are not strong swimmers but have to swim constantly or else they would just sink to the bottom of the water.

HARBOUR SEALS

Harbour seals come ashore to breed, but for about ten months of the year they migrate away from the shore in search of food. The males and females each have their own areas in the ocean and they don't have time to sleep properly, they just rest underwater.

LEATHERBACK TURTLES

Leatherback turtles have been around since the time of the dinosaurs. A leatherback can live for over 100 years, swimming about 15,000 kilometres every year – that's more than a million kilometres in its lifetime!

MONARCH BUTTERFLIES

Monarch butterflies fly at speeds of 25 kilometres per hour and at 2 kilometres above the land. Some travel more than 3,000 kilometres to reach their winter roosting sites in the high snowy mountains of Mexico.

PIED WAGTAILS

In summer these wagtails nest alongside rivers and streams in northern Europe, but in winter they form huge flocks and head into the heart of the cities. It's much warmer there for them and there are plenty of insects for them to eat.

RED DEER

In northern Europe these deer spend the summer on the mountain tops, but when the snow arrives they head downhill where it's warmer. Deer that live near the sea go to the seaside, where they feast on seaweed that has washed ashore.

SARDINES

When the ocean off the coast of Africa grows cold, sardines start to swim to warmer waters up the coast in shoals up to 5 kilometres long, 2 kilometres wide and 30 metres deep. This provides a fish feast for whales, dolphins, seals, sharks and large fish.

WILDEBEEST

Wildebeest follow the rains that make the grass grow, as grass is their main source of food. They take it in turns to sleep so that there are always some wildebeest looking out for predators.